First Words Memory

Children's Reading & Writing Education Books

Speedy Publishing LLC
40 E. Main St. #1156
Newark, DE 19711
www.speedypublishing.com

Aa

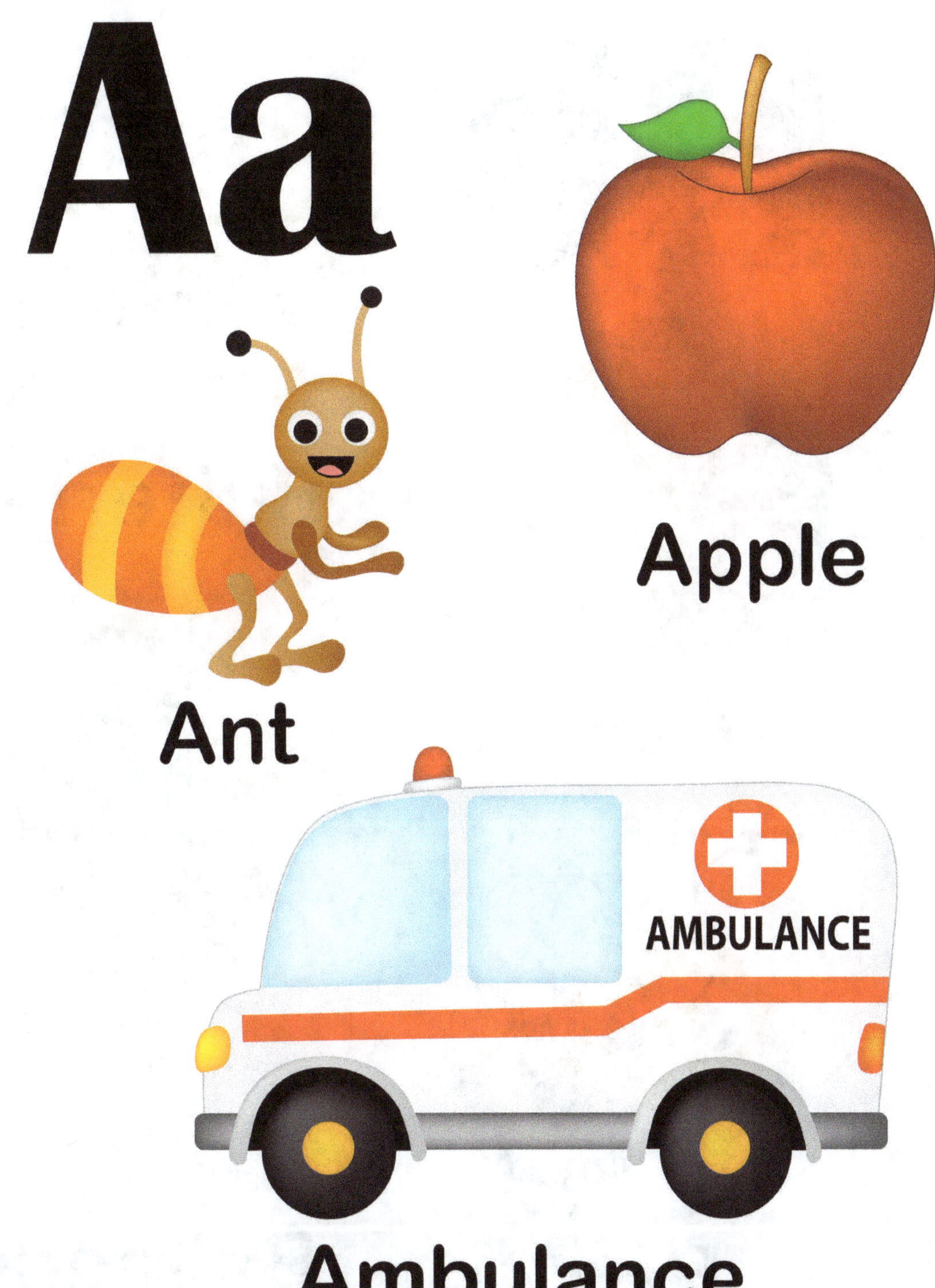

Apple

Ant

Ambulance

Bb

Butterfly

Ball

Balloons

Bee

Cc

Candles

Chicken

Carrot

Cake

Dd

Ee

Elephant

Egg

Envelope

Eggplant

Ff

Fish

Flower

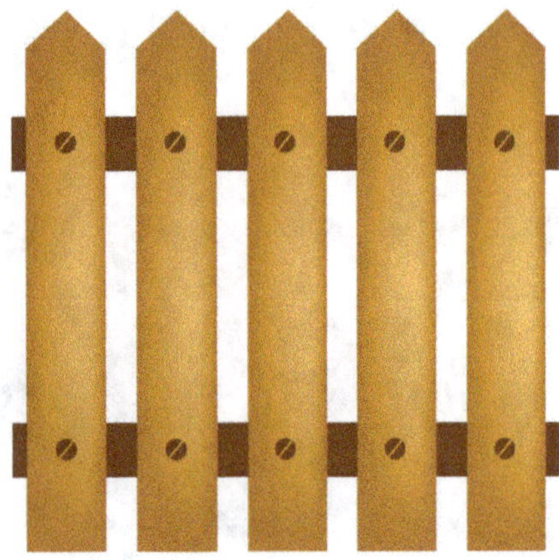

Fence

Frog

Gg

Grapes

Guitar

Gift box

Hh
House
Hat
Hippopotamus
Hammer

Ii
Island
Ice
Ice cream
Igloo

Jj

Jelly beans

Jug

Jelly

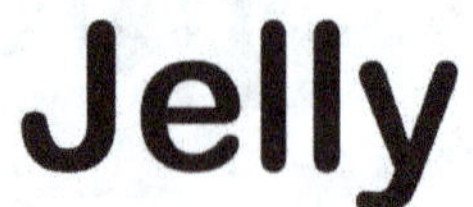

Jelly fish

Kk
Kettle
Kite
Knife
Keyboard

Leaf

Lion

Ladybug

Lamp

Mm

Magnet

Mermaid

Moon

Mushroom

Nn

Nest

Numbers

Notes

Net

Oo
Orange
Owl
Octopus
Onion

Pp

Panda

Pumpkin

Pear

Palette

Qq

Queen

Quetzal

Quilt

Rr
Rainbow
Rattle
Rose
Rocket

Ss
Sun
Sandals
Star
Snowman

Tt

Uu

Utensil

Umbrella

U-turn

UFO

Vv
Vulture
Vase
Van
Vine

Ww
Watermelon
Wand
Whale
Window

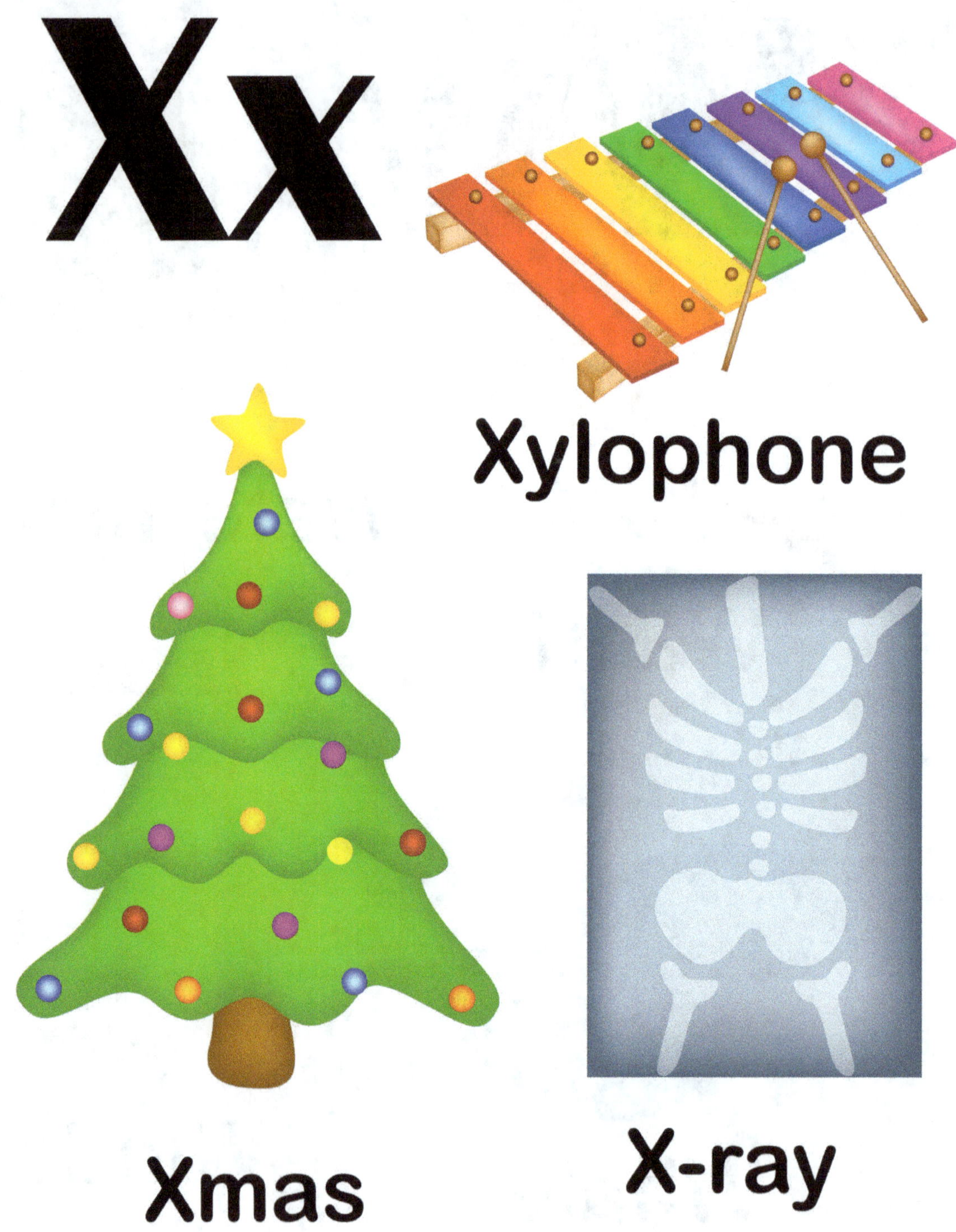
Xx
Xylophone
Xmas
X-ray

Yy

Yoyo

Yacht

Yarn

Yogurt

Zz

Zucchini

Zigzag

Zero

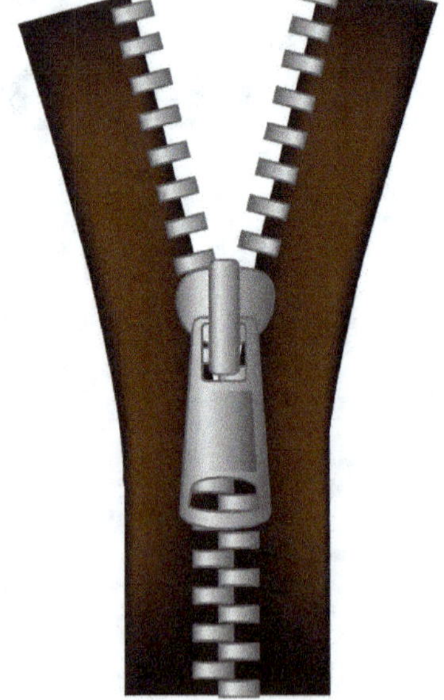

Zipper

Memory Test: Name the object

____

____

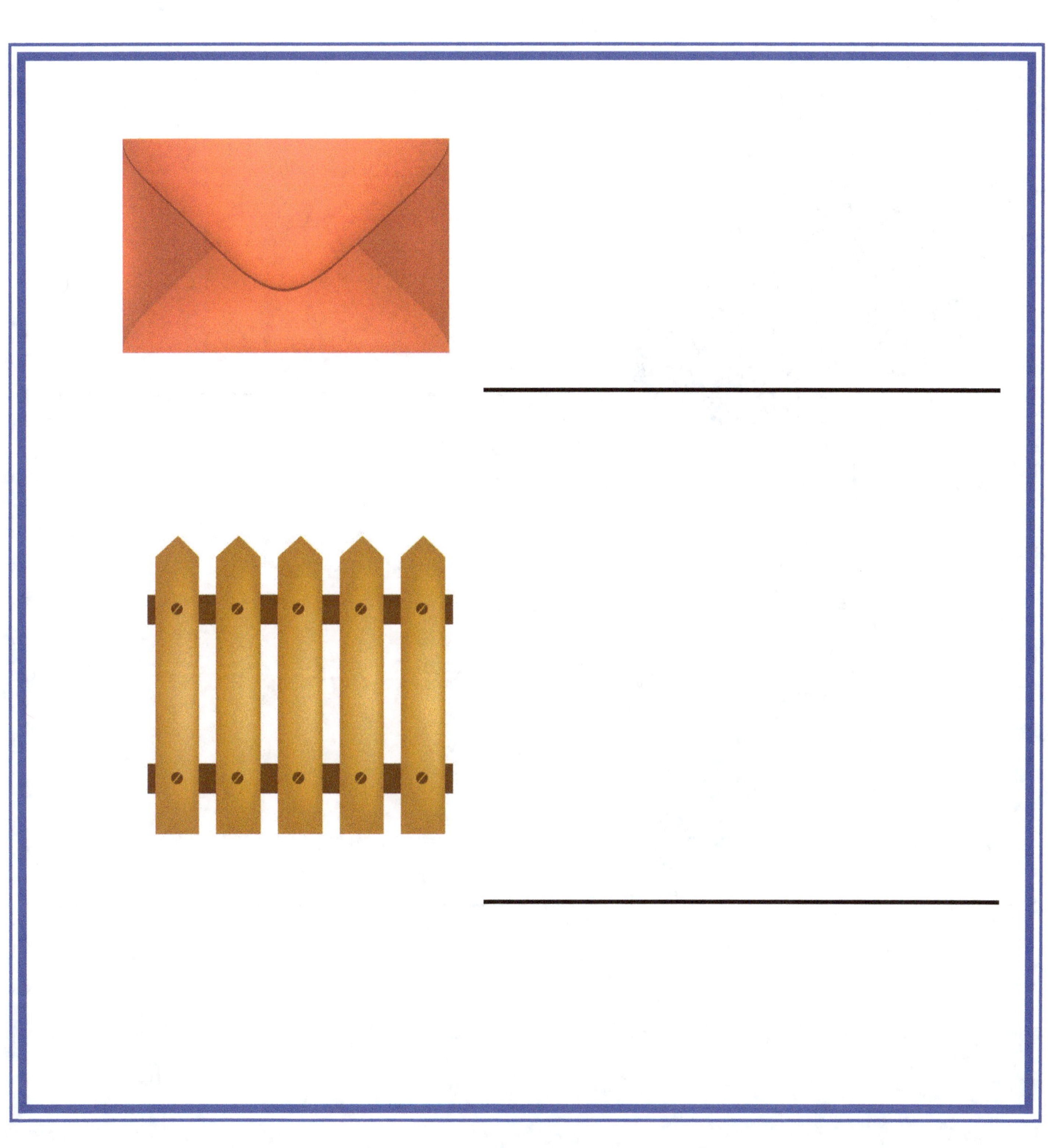

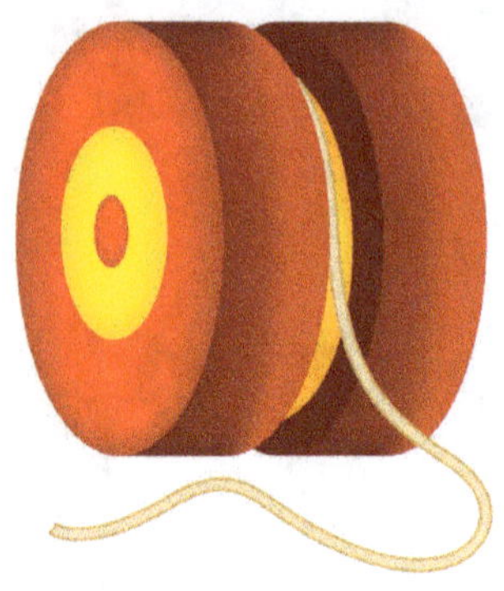

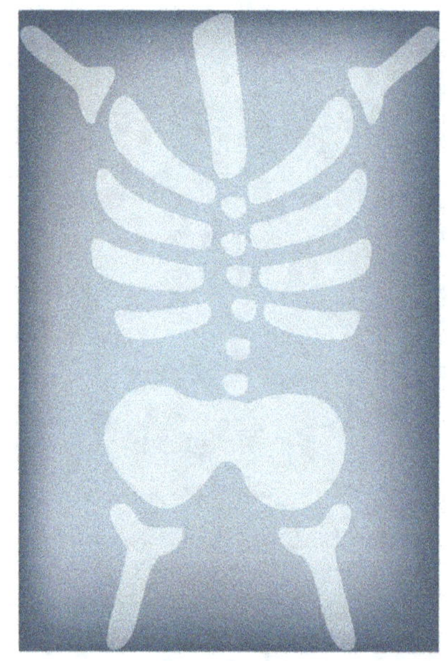

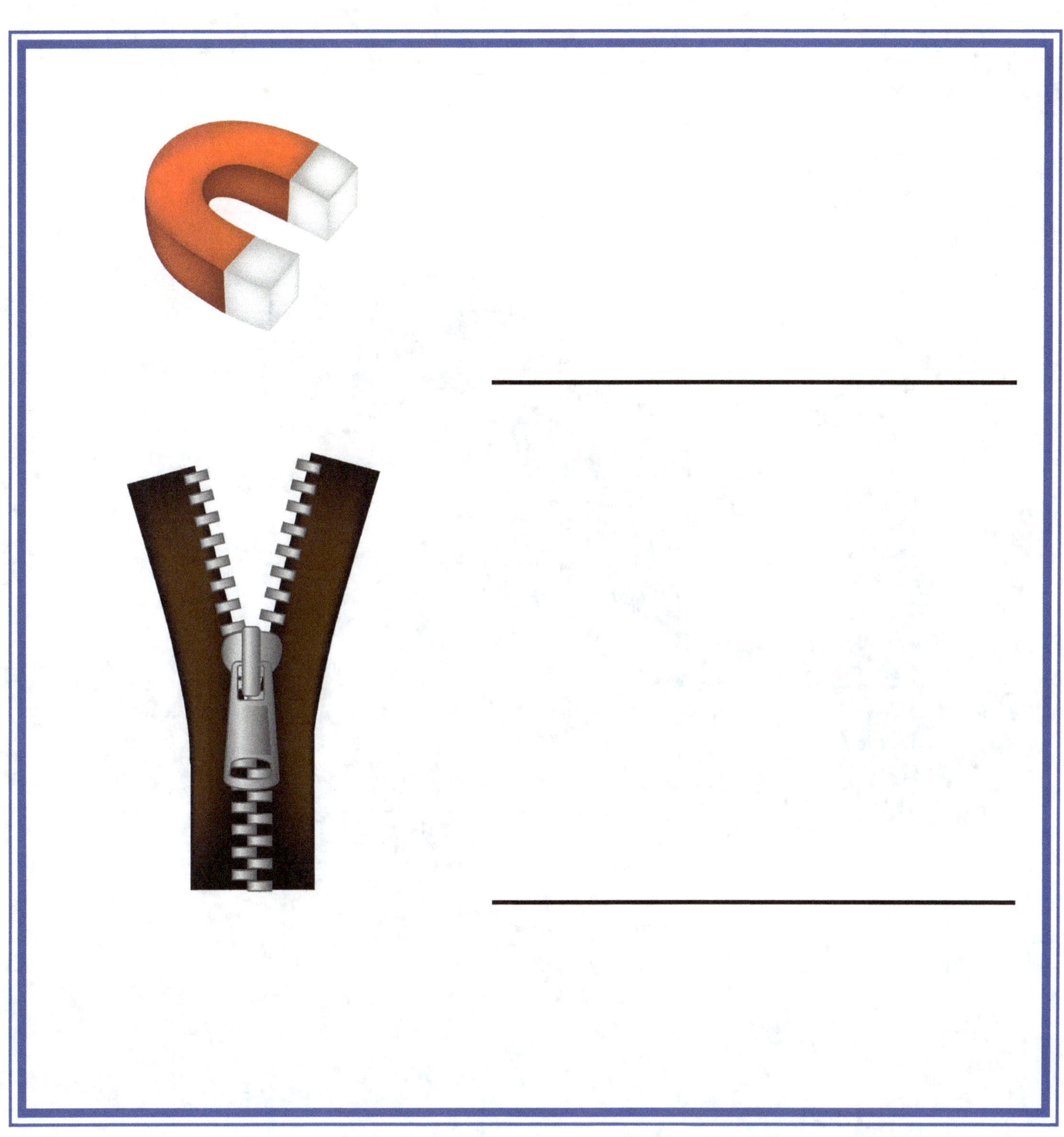

www.ingramcontent.com/pod-product-compliance
Lightning Source LLC
LaVergne TN
LVHW060511170826
845677LV00026B/1713

* 9 7 9 8 8 6 9 4 4 8 9 3 4 *